DANCE WITH THIS BOOK

Start a Revolution with Your Body,

Alone in Your Room.

BY JESS GRIPPO

COPYRIGHT

Jess Grippo Creations, Inc., New York City

Copyright © 2019 Jess Grippo

Cover design by: Jess Grippo

Author photo by: Peter SennYuen

"I had to create a world of my own, like a climate, a country, an atmosphere in which I could breathe, reign, and recreate my-self when destroyed by living.

That, I believe, is the reason for every work of art."

- Anais Nin

You can wait for the stars to align
You can wait for the right kind of sign
You can hope and pray for an answer
You can tiptoe around like a dancer

But no matter the season or time
No matter if you don't have a dime
If there's something you want to do
The power of creation is in YOU.

Because the stars reflect your light
The signs show up with your might
The answer was in you all along
The dancer can choose her song.

- Jess Grippo

get the digital companion:

dancewiththisbook.com

Dance more and feel less lonely with this bonus content:

- guided dance videos

- movement meditations

- online community

- emailed nudges to dance

TABLE OF CONTENTS

introduction: it started with being alone.

My hand popped up immediately as soon as Kyle asked us if anyone had a question. I was part of an audience of 80 people at a workshop with one of my mentors-from-afar, Kyle Cease. I had made the decision to be there that same morning, grabbing a last-minute train ticket upstate, putting myself and the last bit of money I had on the line, and running on what felt like my last fumes. I had finally realized the way I had been functioning was no longer working. I was burnt out, barely making enough money to survive, and struggling to get out of bed on most mornings. (Not an inspiring way to start a book, I know.)

A year prior, I had sat in another audience of Kyle Cease's at his book launch event in NYC. Tears poured out of me as I listened to him talk about the journey that was his book, the dying of his mother, and his new baby on the way. That same morning, I had received the news that my own mother was diagnosed with cancer, setting off the start of what would be of one of the hardest years of my life, leading to the aforementioned breakdown. In an instant, the focus of my world flipped from the work and life I was building for myself in Brooklyn to the care-taking of not one, but two, sick parents in New Jersey, which ultimately got me in touch with a lot of pain inside of myself that had not been looked at. So much of my business and identity crashed during that time. So many of my wounds were revealed. So much of what I thought I had "under control" ended up spinning out of control because I realized I couldn't actually control anything. In hearing Kyle's story that day, I felt hope for my own story. His work - mostly his videos on YouTube - continued to be a guiding light for me as I navigated this path.

And then there I was, a year later, two feet from him as he handed me the mic and invited me up on stage. Within minutes we got to the core of what was blocking my success and happiness: the fear of being alone. As a single woman in her 30s living in a big city, I certainly knew what loneliness felt like, but I had been avoiding being with those uncomfortable feelings — avoiding reconnecting to myself — instead filling up any solo time I had with busy work, Bumble swiping, Netflix watching, and the general hustle and bustle of life in NYC that's so easy to get caught up in. Through Kyle's intuitive questioning, though, I realized being alone was actually where my creativity thrived. Being alone in my room as a child - an only child - was a sanctuary amidst outside chaos, a portal to my imagination where I learned what creativity was. Understanding this melted the fear and made me curious about reconnecting to this part of myself.

Kyle then asked if he could take a video, borrowing someone's iPhone from the audience, and he prompted me to start with, "Hi, I'm Jess, and I'm scared of being alone." After that phrase, I came alive as I spoke to the imaginary person who would someday watch the video:

"...The fact that you're watching this means that something that you're going through is something that I'm going through, too, so there you go! We're both not alone! And as I say this, I feel less alone because I know you're watching this alone in your room, too... so we can just cry together and eat popcorn and watch Dirty Dancing!

"...And you know what else you can do when you're alone? You can make a dance video. If you haven't danced in a while, you don't have to go spend hours of your day or get "in shape" again or make yourself go to that class and try to kick your leg way up there... You don't have to do that. You know why? Because there's a dance studio in your room right now. In your aloneness there is a dance studio. Grab your phone. Put on the video camera. Put on some music. See what happens when you let yourself be a dancer because you freakin' want to, alone in your room. See how you come alive. See how you transform that loneliness into something that is creative expression. Something that will reach people. Something that I think will change the world. So it starts with one dance video. It starts with you being alone. You're exactly where you need to be. Turn this off and go dance."

(It's on YouTube still, in case you're curious: "<u>I've been scared of being alone. How bout you?</u>")

On the train ride home, I wrote the first four chapters of this book you're holding. It poured out of me — a complete rewrite of the book I had been trying to complete for three years. Through this process, I fell back in love with the mystery of my own creativity and realized it was worth much more than all the distractions I had been creating to avoid it.

What followed was NOT a linear path to completing the book, by the way. I had to do a lot of inner work to get to the place where I could make the time and find the inspiration to complete it, let alone share it. I had to face my demons, as they say. (Still facing them!) I had to let myself spiral into an emotional tornado of relationship drama that left me broken down. I was slapped in the face with the reality of how much I was seeking validation and fearing abandonment, replaying old programming from my childhood, and not tending to the child within myself who really just wanted to dance and be free.

This book is a result of coming home to myself, of realizing that if I wanted to make a change in the world, I had to first address myself and make peace with being alone in my room, once again. When I stopped filling the void with app swiping and over-working, I actually had space for both myself and for the creative muses who were dying to dance through me. I remembered I am enough, my dancing matters, and that embracing myself and my dance might just be the path to my freedom.

May this book be part of the spark that invites the muses into your room, too.

Why listen to me?

Well, you don't have to listen to me, of course. But if you picked up this book, I thought maybe you'd want to know a little more of the history that got me to the point of writing it.

Although I've danced for most of my life, I spent most of that time feeling totally disconnected from my body: trying to control it, to get it to do more pirouettes or higher arabesques, to shrink it, to force it beyond its limitations. In other words, trying to fit it into a mold that just wasn't natural for me. (hello, classical ballet!)

I left the ballet world at 19 years old, went on to study a mix of psychology, sociology, and gender studies at NYU, and then ended up in a 9-5 job that had nothing to do with what I studied or was interested in. (hello, the-fate-of-most-people-with-psychology majors!)

After addressing my lingering health issues — PCOS, which I began to heal with the help of Alisa Vitti — I made my way into a career in the holistic health world, joining forces with Alisa to become a women's hormonal health coach on her team at Flo Living. (hello, doing-something-that-helped-people! Which I soon realized was what I had been craving.)

For years I pushed dance aside until the calling became hard to ignore.

As I started to dabble around with ways to dance again (including unabashedly performing "All That Jazz" at every karaoke opportunity I could find), I couldn't face going back into a traditional classroom setting. Just thinking about it felt like torture — way too intimidating for some-one like me, who was almost seven years out of practice — so I didn't do it. Instead, I started dancing in my own way: improvising in my bedroom or at hidden places in the park, eventually making my own dance videos and shar-ing them with others. I was discovering dance in a new way: as a fulfilling creative outlet where my body, my voice, and my soul were free to move and express. And it all started by giving myself permission to dance alone in my room.

That was back in 2009, and the rest is an ever-evolving history in the making. While the original idea for this book was to write it for the You who would eventually read it, I ended up writing it for me. I ended up scrapping the first version (which I had worked on for YEARS, by the way) and rewrote it on that train ride home because I had to tell myself all these things again. And in the telling and retelling of it, I got back to myself and to the original roots of where my dance revival started — you guessed it: alone in my room. In retrospect, I think that was the only way this book would be able to really speak to you authentically.

A few notes before you dive in:

The chapters can be read in order or at random, depending on which section calls to you. At the close of each one is a "dance prompt," i.e. a guided direction for you to take your dance in. These prompts are meant to be explored alone in your room. No studio space, leotards, fancy dance pants, or anything else required.

I highly recommend actually dancing these prompts, not just reading them, as they will anchor in the concepts and bring you into more connection with your body and soul — which is the point of all this anyway!

I also encourage you to go to dancewiththisbook.com to get the digital companion to the book, and join me and the rest of the community online. Although you may start out alone in your room, you don't have to feel isolated. There are tons of dance rebels out there, just like you and me, who are dancing into their answers one step at a time and looking to connect with others along the way. I created programs and community to support you in this unfolding, so don't be shy! (or be shy, but still reach out ;)

With that, I invite you to turn the page and see for yourself. Let's begin this journey of dancing alone, together.

chapter 1: you don't have to do it "right."

It's no coincidence that people looooove those videos. You know the ones. The ones of the little girl on stage at her dance recital, totally jamming out to her own tune, totally out of sync with the rest of the line-up, and in full-on, self-expression beast mode.

A question for you: if we all love that little girl so much, why do we hold ourselves to such standards of perfection when it comes to getting our own dance moves "right"? Even worse, why do we hold ourselves back from dancing at all?

The dance videos getting the most love on the internet are the ones that are the most authentic and that remind each of us of our free-spirited self. You know, the one we've each locked away.

I'll start this baby off by saying this: there is no "right" way to dance. Sure, there are specific techniques and styles of dance you can learn, and they have certain rules and steps, a"right" way of doing things, so to speak. But there are a lot of other ways to dance, too. There are left ways. And backwards ways. And on-the-verge-of-a-breakdown ways. (Believe me, I've been there!)

And because this book is called, <u>Dance with this Book</u>, not <u>How To Perfect Your Dance Technique</u>, we're going to be focusing on all those OTHER ways you can dance.

The kind of dancing I want to talk about here ranges from the grit to the great, the growling to the glory. It's about moving life through that beautiful vessel you call your body. This book is about finding YOUR rhythm, about connecting to a place inside yourself that will ultimately help you in connecting to the outside world, too. It's about healing yourself through one of the most primal medicines we have: dance.

I promise, the dance is in you! Even if you've told yourself (or have been told by others) that you have no rhythm or grace, or that you missed your chance because you never made that Rockettes audition, dance is a primal, natural part of YOU. And when it comes to you dancing your dance, there's no such thing as "getting it right."

By the way, just because I know this, doesn't mean I don't still think about "getting it right" sometimes. Even as I write this book, the thought crosses my mind: "I hope I'm getting it right." I imagine if I messed up this first chapter, you'd close the book forever, you'd hate me, and you'd give up dancing all over again!

Eek! Perfectionism is a bitch, am I right?

So let's make a deal; I won't let it stop me if you won't let it stop you either, k?

To that end, I'm granting myself permission: permission to "mess up," to be wild, to be myself. I promise this book will be more fun for you to read that way. (And I know I'll get a lot more out of it, too.) In giving ourselves permission to dance and live full out, we remember who we are.

That's why, as you start dancing with this book, I'm going to ask you to also give yourself permission. Remember, there is no "getting it right" here.

Now before we go any further, let's address the dancing elephant in the room: you haven't been dancing as much as you want to, but you've somehow found time to read this book.

This begs the question: if you can make time to read this, why don't you just dance instead? Why *read* about dancing instead of actually dancing?

[I'll give you space to think about that one...]

Here's my guess (and it's part of why I made time to write the damn thing):

It's hard to make time for dance, especially when you've been away from it for awhile. There are a lot of reasons not to, I get it! You're busy. You're tired. There's not enough space in your apartment or enough time for you to get your butt to a class. A book, on the other hand, *that* you can make space for. You can be with a book in silence on a train or in bed without even needing to engage your body. Score!

There's another reason why you might have reached for a book about dance: we need each other's stories.

We need to know we're not isolated in our challenges and growth, and we glimpse that through the shared words of another on the creative path. If we try to do it all by ourselves, we'll most likely quit way too early when our inner critic kills the dream. Isolated, we start believing that voice in our head saying, "change is not possible," "we're too old to start dancing again," and "no one cares anyway!" Or maybe the voice is saying, "it's selfish to dance." Isolated, our intuition is drowned out by our addictions to these critical thoughts -- or our addictions to other things. So let's not go there. You don't have to be isolated in this. (Alone is different than isolated.) You've got me here. And you've got these words.

The words of so-called strangers have helped me more times than I can count. Think of this book as a packet of stories from a caring stranger that you can read whenever you're feeling alone and in need of a creative spark. Reading this book (and if you're brave, following its prompts), is a powerful way to get out of your head, which is how we *really* begin disrupting the critical thought patterns holding us hostage.

You know what I mean about being held hostage, right? How you'll get the urge to dance, but your mind finds a way to shut the impulse down before you've even had a chance to fully entertain the possibility. There are so many things that might come up for you in that space:

- How selfish it is to take time for yourself when so-and-so needs you, there are bills to pay, and a million things are hanging out on your to-do list.
- How you're so rusty and out of shape, why should you even bother because it probably won't feel good anyway.
- How Jimmy made fun of you when you did The Butterfly that one time at your 6th grade dance and you never want to experience that kind of ridicule again.

Maybe that last one's just me. Regardless, I'm sure you get it. The list of reasons not to dance goes on and on. What does *your* mind tell you?

Jot down your top 3 reasons to NOT dance here:

Whatever you wrote, what *I'm* here to tell you is this: these thoughts are the biggest block to you dancing freely, and they probably won't go away any time soon. That inner critical voice in your head just comes with being human. Seriously, we all have one, and it's main job is to keep us from doing anything that feels scary, new, or even exciting. Why? Because it likes to be in control and stay safe - and that often looks like doing the same ol' things you usually do, even if they are no longer serving your bigger purpose.

The good news is, I'm not asking you to audition for Dancing with the Stars or step into an Advanced Contemporary Jazz class at Broadway Dance Center in Manhattan tomorrow. I'm asking you to dance alone, in your room, where no one is watching. Where it's just you, your body, and some music.

The beauty of this approach--of dancing alone in your room where no one is watching--is that, like I mentioned earlier, you really can give yourself full permission to mess up, do it "wrong," to be fully yourself, and to dance the dance that is in your heart, in your soul, in your heart AND soul...possibly to the tune of "Heart and Soul," the song? You know, just like Tom Hanks dancing like a child on the giant floor piano in the movie *Big*.

Now I'm not saying that you won't feel moved to dance somewhere *outside your room* while reading this book.

You might be inspired to get back into ballet, take up belly dancing or burlesque for the first time, or join the local Thriller flash mob. To be clear, I'm not knocking the idea of doing a specific kind of dance. If you crave that kind of structure and learning environment, that's wonderful. Do it!

Regardless of what kind of dancing you choose, this book is meant to enhance your personal dance journey. And if you don't know yet what specifically is calling you, this book is here to help you get clarity. It's designed to open you up to your inner experience so that you can feel more empowered to dance YOUR dance in both your inner and outer world. Sound good?

I completely understand that dancing alone might still cause you to feel self-conscious or weird. Stuff comes up! You know, *feelings*. This is fantastic! I promise. Believe it or not, you *want* feelings to come up. Allowing yourself to feel whatever it is you discover beneath the surface as you move your body (or even think about moving your body) will totally free you. (More on that later.)

If you feel awkward, stiff, or even bored when you start, don't worry. This is NORMAL, and it's definitely no reason to stop. The nature of creative expression is that it takes time. We need practice to find our flow, and often, we experience resistance to getting going. Remember for your at-home dance practice, it's all about showing up. Failing is your friend. Flailing is your friend. Falling is your friend. All these things will help you find YOU. And your commitment to showing up is all it takes. Be willing to get it wrong. Just take the first step. And then the next. And then the next.

While we're on the subject of first steps, I'll admit it: they can be challenging to take. Though the concept of beginning is quite simple, that doesn't mean it's always easy. Why? Because of that resistance I mentioned a minute ago. Believe me, if you're anything like I am, you'll come up with a million other things you could do instead of dance when the prompts in this book invite you to. You'll feel tired, you'll get distracted, you'll put this book down and turn on Netflix.

Taking that first step is challenging because it's a pattern interruption. Even if it's just a minute of dancing alone in your bedroom. That first step is about you choosing something outside your usual, and for the egoic mind, that can be scary. It causes a shift from your mind being in control to your body and soul leading the way, opening you up for the vast unknown in you to speak! (Dramatic, I know.) I mean it, though. That one minute of moving into the unknown, or of even thinking about dancing, can bring up a lot, including all the shitty memories that are stored in your body that you don't even realize are there. It can also bring up all the rules and conditioning you've internalized about how it is or isn't ok to move. So, be gentle with you. And remember, taking that first step can also bring you release and joy, especially if you've been comfortable feeling stuck or being busy.

Taking that first step in your dance journey is an act of trust. It's you trusting you'll be safe when all of a sudden, you imagine a ghost of a dance partner extending their hand and inviting you to follow along. Even though you've never met them before, even though you can't see them, and even though you have no idea where they are leading or what your body will do if you follow, you say "yes."

I've got news for you: that ghost dance partner is actually YOU. (Bummer! I know. I was hoping it would be Patrick Swayze, too.) It's the part of you that has been there since you were little, since the days when you danced freely around your room with no concern for what anyone else thought. It's the part of you that is so freakin' excited to see you move your own body, wild and free.

I invite you to meet this part of you. Greet yourself with curiosity as you take that first step. Because nobody puts you in the corner, baby.

Ready or not?

Go on, take the first dance step! I'll see you in the next chapter.

→ **DANCE BREAK!**

Here's your prompt for this chapter: Dance it "wrong."

Take some sort of dance movement that you know or kind of know, or don't really know at all but like to imitate from YouTube videos, and mess it up. Maybe it's the Macarena or maybe it's the final scene of Flashdance. Whatever floats your dance boat. As you dance, make it all about messing it up, doing it "wrong," and seeing how totally far from "right" you can actually be. Discover how you can make two left feet the most fun thing ever.

---

chapter 2: be your own dj.

Have you ever been to a dance class or wedding or club where people around you are totally jamming out, but you're just standing there doing fake fist-pumps, trying to figure out why you're not having fun? It's probably because it's house music. (Just kidding, I don't hate house music. I just like joking about how I do.) Seriously though, it could be that the music playing isn't grabbing your soul. It's not pulling your heart out of your chest and dragging you onto the dance floor, and let's be real, it's not easy to dance if the music doesn't move you. It's also not easy to dance if the environment you're in feels uncomfortable or judgy or too exposed. Yet, when we find ourselves not dancing, we often think WE are the ones at fault. We blame ourselves for not getting out there rather than seeing the situation for what it is: an environmental or soundtrack mismatch.

So what do we do? Well, for many of us, our autopilot is programmed to shut down. We either dance along to what's playing, totally unenthused or self-conscious, or we find ourselves being a wallflower and thinking thoughts like, "I shouldn't dance at all." The trouble is, just because one dance environment isn't working for us, we often start believing we are the problem. Or worse, that dance is the problem. What would happen if, instead of shutting down, we began wondering, "What kind of dance environment would really move me? Is it something I could find or create myself?"

This is where you being your own DJ comes in.

When you're the DJ, you're in charge. You not only get to choose the music you dance to, but you also get to choose where the dancing happens and with whom. Unlike the dance classes of your past, there's no critical, controlling dance teacher standing in the doorway, forcing you to listen to Tchaikovsky as you learn the dance of the snowflakes. No! This is YOUR dance life now, and you get to spin it however you choose.

As your own DJ, you also get to decide whether you'll go on tour or stay put. While it can be really fun to take your dancing out into the world, I'm a really big advocate of starting out alone in your room and staying there for as long as feels good. In your own space, you can choose whatever music you want to dance to, and you can feel safe knowing that no one is judging you for your choices or forcing you to follow along with the flock. Your private dance floor is where you can redefine the dance rules and rediscover who you are. You might even choose a DJ name! Why not?!

When it comes to music, I encourage you to experiment. You might have playlists you already love, or you might be searching for more musical inspiration. If you're not sure what music moves you, spend some time browsing around on Spotify or Pandora or wherever the kids find their music these days.

Music, like creativity energy, has an endless supply. If choosing music makes you anxious because it triggers your indecisive tendency and you feel like you have no idea where to begin, I feel you. I've been there! In fact, one of the biggest blocks I moved through when I first felt the desire to start leading dance experiences was the fear that I wouldn't be able to pick "good" music. I was afraid my playlists would be lame and that people would judge me. I was convinced I just wasn't cool enough to pick the "right" tunes, and for a while, it really had me stuck.

(Do you see? There I go again, trying to get it "right"! See how deeply ingrained that is?)

At a certain point, I got tired of that excuse and I decided to just choose *something* and go with it. I centered that first dance experience around an 80s-inspired Flashdance playlist. After all, Irene Cara had kept me company many times alone in my room, and while not everyone might be into the 80s thing, those who were found me. And they loved it!

The point is, there are no rules when it comes to music selections for your dancing, but you do have to start *somewhere*. Dabble in musical options until you land on what moves you. Ask for music recommendations from your

Facebook friends (or your real life friends). Compile playlists, make lists of the styles of music you want to learn more about, and don't be afraid to leave it to chance and just hit "shuffle" if you're feeling stuck. Sometimes, playing with a track you might not have chosen yourself is just the thing to open you up, and an unexpected song can lead us all to places we didn't anticipate.

If you're really not feeling the music or just wanting something new, dancing in silence is always an option. Sometimes the beat of your heart, the sound of your floor creaking, or the soothing rush of your own breath is all you need to hear as your body begins to move. Being with your body without a musical soundtrack creates an opportunity to listen to yourself and your body's wisdom in a new way. What will your body do when given the chance to make its own music? What happens if you create movement first, and then add music after? Try it out and see! There's so much to discover, regardless of which path you choose.

Remember, nothing is static in dance or in life. As you redefine who you are as a dancer and a human, your musical choices will likely shift and evolve to mirror the ever-changing ebbs and flows of your life. As long as you allow your music and your dance to be a response to how you feel inside, you'll always find the musical match for what longs to be expressed.

→ DANCE BREAK!

Here's your prompt for this chapter: **The Dance Shuffle**

It's always interesting to be open to suggestion. Just for kicks, don't decide yourself on which music to dance to. Instead, let your iPod/radio/phone/laptop do the deciding for you! (Not sure why I started that list out with two devices that probably 99.99999% of you haven't used since 2003 or 1993, respectively, but there it is.) You can think of this exercise like the tarot card reading of dance. Just like with a deck of tarot cards, you shuffle, pull one out at random , and receive a message you needed to hear. In this case, hit shuffle on your playlist (or go to the radio station of a song you like) and see what message the music has for you! Maybe the lyrics will speak to you directly. Maybe the tempo or beat will ignite something that's been wanting to move through you. Or maybe you'll just feel good trying out something totally unexpected and new.

1. *Open up your music library/playlist/whatever and hit "shuffle."*
2. *Let 3 songs play in a row. Give yourself permission to hit skip if you really need to, but do your best to give each random song a chance -- even*

if it's not something you would usually choose
or if you feel awkward at first.

3. Allow yourself time to work it out and get into a
    groove by committing to dancing through all 3
    songs. This is the equivalent of about 10 minutes
    of dancing, which is a good amount of time be-
    cause often, it takes more than a minute or two
    to really get the energy moving.

Want to take it to the next level? Try doing a page or
two of free-writing after your Dance Shuffle. It's a
great way to unblock any creative stuckness and to
get more in touch with subconscious thoughts and
feelings that will surface as you begin allowing your
body the freedom to speak.

chapter 3: you can't stop the feeling.

Justin Timberlake might've flopped during his 2018 Super Bowl Halftime performance (my friend's three-year-old was caught on video saying, "Turn it off. Nothing is happening."), but he did nail it with this song:

"Can't Stop The Feeling!"

If we think of feelings like invisible but very real creatures that live inside and even on top of us, it's easy to see that while we might try to stop the feelings from being felt, we never really can. When feelings aren't released or allowed to move through us in the form of creativity or emotional expression, they stay stuck to us and in us, weighing us down, stifling our energy, and preventing us from living as our biggest selves. They may come out sideways when we least expect it, turning an otherwise lovely family dinner into a scene from *The Exorcist*.

He truth is, whether or not we choose to acknowledge our feeling monsters, they are always there. So why do we ignore them? Why do we not want them to be known?

A big part of it is societal. Clearly we're all raised differently, but there's something about our modern day world that rewards the mentally-focused, goal-oriented, do-do-

do, productive-at-all-times mode, and encourages us to sacrifice our well-being for the sake of keeping up. Tired? Doesn't matter, keep going, have a latte. Feeling sick? There's a pill for that. Feeling sad? There's a pill for that, too. When we keep moving towards what's next and next and next, we lose touch with our internal wisdom; we learn how to keep ourselves numb.

And so we bury our feeling monsters--whether on purpose or unconsciously--because it can be scary to feel them. We choose to watch 34 episodes of *How I Met Your Mother* on Netflix or stuff our faces with the latest craft beer or ice cream (or both!) instead of allowing a few minutes to really be with ourselves and feel what's going on inside. We hold back our tears and laughter and screams because it doesn't feel appropriate to let them out in the moment, when what we really need is to let those little monsters loose! What we need is to laugh or yell or cry out the heartbreak--whatever's moving through us--so we can come back to a place of ease and freedom in our bodies rather than trying to keep it all in.

Over the years, I've experienced myself and have also had clients share feelings like: "I'm scared to access my grief or anger. What if it doesn't ever go away? What if I get stuck in that low-feeling place? What if it lasts forever and I'm sad for the rest of my life?"

When we're used to burying our feelings, it's easy to imagine that will happen...that we will be overwhelmed by what's lurking beneath the surface. But here's the thing: when we resist feeling what's there, that scary emotion persists. Not accessing and expressing our emotions leads to numbness, stuckness, lethargy, and depression. Yes, when we unleash the feelings and emotions that want to come out, it can be really painful at first. But once you get through it, you often feel different afterward.

That's not to say the feeling monster will be gone forever after you release it once. It might come back. Especially grief - it's not something we cry out once and it's over. We can continue to honor it and feel it and let it move through us time and time again whenever it comes up, like laughter. We go to a comedy show because we want to laugh, but we're not scared we'll keep laughing for the rest of our lives, right? We enjoy the night, we get the belly laughs going, we leave feeling lighter and smiling more. It shifts us. And maybe that's the end of it, or maybe, a few hours or days or even weeks later, we remember something from that night and it activates our laughter all over again.

An important note: we're not always ready and equipped to handle tough emotions on our own. If you're in the middle of a dance break or spending time with yourself and stuff comes up that makes you uncomfortable, it's ok to push pause if you need to. It's ok to switch to a happy song if you really can't handle the sad one today. That's where therapists and coaches come into play, as we are not meant to process tough stuff completely on our own. It's ok to ask for support. It's ok to be witnessed in your pain and in your healing. (And if you *are* seeking more one-on-one support, please reach out.)

So how does this all relate to dance? When we dance, we are giving our bodies space and time to speak, and therefore, we are allowing the feeling monsters that are living in there to potentially be heard.

Here's the thing - you never know what's going to come out of your dance practice, just like you can't know what will come of trusting yourself to acknowledge and express your feelings. The truth is, it's not up to you to know. It's up to you to show up for it and to create the space for what wants to move through you.

Rather than letting the thinking/planning part of your brain distract you and distance you from your body, use it instead to plan for how you can set boundaries in your time and space to make room for your body. That might mean letting the people you live with know that between 7 and 8 pm on Thursday nights you can't be bothered because that's your sacred dance time. Or maybe it means creating a communal dance break with them once a week. Or maybe you decide to turn off your phone in the morning and not look at it until you've danced. There are all kinds of ways to use your mind to set healthy boundaries that serve your body. Play around with it until you discover what works for you!

In that process of being with yourself, you'll begin to uncover what kind of movement and feelings might want to be expressed. Maybe some days you'll roll around on the floor and that's all you can do. Maybe other days you'll jump up and down screaming and letting out a ton of energy. It doesn't matter what it looks like. It just matters that you move. (Or be still in a cocoon of blankets if it happens to be a day when you need to slow down. Because let's be real, we all have those days.)

Whatever you've got going on, in the process of being with yourself and your body, those feeling monsters that have been clinging to you will start to unravel and loosen their grip. They will come alive in their own way through your expression so they can be released. You'll dance them on out into the universe so that they won't hold you hostage anymore. And as you dance with them, opening up your creative channels and unclogging the backlog of crap that's been piling up, you unstick yourself. And maybe, just maybe, you realize you're not afraid of monsters anymore.

→ **DANCE BREAK!**

Here's your prompt for this chapter: **Monster Flashdance**

Begin by visualizing your "Feeling Monsters" all around or inside of you. If you have scarfs or fabric available, tie them around you (gently of course - be safe!), and feel what comes up. Allow yourself to stand or lie there and be still at first. Put on music (or not) and dance with these monsters. Maybe let them loose or peel off any layers you've tied on. See what it is that they want you to do. Envision them coming off of you or dancing with you, but don't rush the process. Spend time with the monsters to feel and understand them first, then release them, listening to them as you do. As a bonus, do some free writing afterward and see what comes through after you set them free.

chapter 4: rear end it.

Quick, give yourself a tap on the butt! Or a few taps. Both cheeks. (Really, do it now.) This is like applauding yourself for choosing to dance with this book. (You rock!)

The tap-on-the-butt is also here to get you present to this part of your body. Not just your butt, actually, but your hips and pelvis, too. And alllllll the parts on the inside.

If we were speaking in energetic terms, we'd be referring to your first and second chakras, the energy centers at the base of your spine and just below the navel. This clearly isn't a book about chakras, so I don't want to dive too deeply into them (though there are plenty of excellent books out there on the subject if your interest is piqued). What you need to know for our purposes is that these lower chakras hold some really juicy stuff. The root chakra (base of your spine) is where security and belonging live, and the sacral chakra (just below the navel) is where creativity and sexuality reside.

I sometimes like to think of the root chakra as extending out into the legs and feet, as in your actual roots and connectors to the ground beneath you. Starting out a dance practice by connecting to your physical roots and imagining their deepening into the earth beneath you, holding you and supporting, can be very powerful in setting the stage for a sense of safety and connection before you start moving. From this place of groundedness, our bodies can feel secure to let energy move throughout the system. Once we are safe and secure, we can access and move more of our creative energy from the lower belly/pelvic area, aka second chakra.

In 2005, Shakira told us, "My hips don't lie." Whatever year you're reading this book, let me remind you that this still stands true for each of us. If we're locked up in these lower areas of our bodies--physically, energetically, emotionally, spiritually, whatever!--it interferes with our ability to live our lives fully-expressed. We can use dance as a tool to open ourselves up again. Why? So that our energy can really start flowing. So that we can feel grounded and creative. So that we can be secure and flip the switch to turn our bodies on.

For a moment, let's entertain the idea that this lower region of your body actually does have to do with a sense of belonging, groundedness, security, creativity, sexuality. Tell me, what does your unique movement in this area of your body say about those things?

Can you wiggle your hips? Or do you feel locked up? If you let your butt lead the dance, where will it take you? Does any emotion come up as you begin to get things moving down there? What do you feel? What happens if you place your hands on your belly while you move? What's hiding out in those spaces waiting to be witnessed and released? Can you feel it to heal it?

Take a moment to write out the answers to those questions if it feels like a juicy topic for you right now.

I once worked with a client, we'll call him Kris, who was referred to me in his search for dance instructors. In his own words, he shared with me that he had felt disconnected from his body and emotions his whole life, and that he wanted someone to guide him in getting back in touch with himself. Despite his outward appearance of success, there was a nagging feeling of emptiness inside of him, and he wasn't quite sure how to address it even though he noticed it was creating a wall between him and his family, as well as in his relationships with his colleagues.

When we began working together, we quickly discovered the most challenging thing for Kris was moving his hips. We worked together on basic isolations, starting to create neural connections between those hips and his brain. We also talked about the emotions that came up along the way as he gained more range of motion. One session, we spent almost our entire hour dancing through a lot of Kris' pent up emotions, including anger. He experienced a huge release in that session, and it opened him up to crying for the first time in years.

What Kris experienced in getting to know his hips and learning how to move them goes way beyond him being able to hold his own on the dance floor. As he got more powerfully in touch with those energy centers of the first and second chakras, he also began carrying himself differently, with more confidence. The way he interacted with his wife and coworkers shifted too - the wall began to crumble. I invite you to get into conversation with your own hips. You never know what kind of walls you might crumble in your own life by really moving them.

Remember that communication with our bodies is a process that is ever unfolding. It feels important to mention that having breakthroughs with our dancing doesn't mean everything is solved forever. Sometimes, two steps forward leads to one step back. Just as we can value our rear-ends and the chakral wisdom they contain, we can also value the moments when we take a turn towards the rear and backslide a bit.

All this is to say, don't worry if you have days where you feel like you're stuck in reverse with your dance practice or with life. If you've been dancing regularly and then you go for a week without moving your body, it's ok! You're not bad and nothing is wrong. You can always start dancing again.

Stepping backwards into old patterns is sometimes necessary to remind us of where we truly want to go next. If you catch yourself in a pattern that feels familiar and that you know is not getting you where you need to go, practice being kind to yourself. Instead of resisting what's happening, try dancing with it. Rather than pushing yourself forward into something new, be with the experience you're having right now. Be with it in movement. Dance out the feeling of being stuck on the loop of chaos and self-blame. Really embody it. See how the energy wants to be expressed through your body, without words. Go deeper with it. Take up space. Get bigger. Or get smaller, if that's what you're feeling. See if your movement naturally wants to evolve into a different pattern or direction, or just follow your rear-end. Trust your body to go there. When you relax your thinking and let movement lead the way, it creates opportunities to feel into the body's knowing, or as I like to call it, to dance into our answers.

→ **DANCE BREAK!**

Here's your prompt for this chapter: **Rearview Mirror**

Get into some high-quality booty shaking during your dance break today, focusing on the backside of your body and on backwards movement. Put on music that really makes you move. Place your hands on your hips and/or lower belly so that you really become aware of your lower body. Imagine you have eyes in the back of your head or hips and close your front eyes, perhaps, allowing whatever you sense behind you to drive your movement. You might even want to lean against a wall or lay on the floor and move against a surface to feel your back body even more.

chapter 5: follow your heart (in a non-cliche way).

Follow your heart? Really, Jess?

It's one of those phrases we hear *so* often. On Hallmark cards, on t-shirts in the junior's section of Kohl's, in the autographs section of your high school yearbook. And I think there's a reason this phrase scratches the itch of our pre-teen and teenage consciousness...it's the last whisper of childhood hope we latch onto before our heads fully take over, steering us down the logical path of What You're Supposed To Do As a Responsible Adult.

We may also hear the phrase "follow your heart" as adults, and while we know we "should" be following our hearts, who really has time for that? We're mostly stuck in our heads by that point, so the message barely penetrates. It might manage to sprinkle a *little* hope in there so we still buy the tank top for our ten-year-old niece because we want *her* to remember. She's still in the heart realm and we believe in her and maybe she won't forget like we did.

For the skeptical adult part of me, the idea of following your heart evokes a blindly passionate, overly optimistic, quit-your-job-to-become-a-singer/songwriter   mindset that really only works well in the movies.

Then why would I write a chapter in my book about it, you might ask?

Well, in dance, I like to use the phrase in a literal way to avoid all those other (sometimes cheesy) associations.

When I say, "Follow your heart," I mean listening to that beating thing in your chest.

If you still yourself enough to actually listen to your heart-beat and feel it in your body, how would it compel you to move? When you connect to the natural rhythm within you, the same beat you spent nine months cozied up next to in the womb, the same beat that keeps you alive and connects you to a common song of humanity, do you remember? Do you remember that it's really *that* simple? That you can be soothed by this sound anytime your head starts talking too much? That you actually DO have rhythm, even if you've been telling yourself you don't?

If you feel distanced from your childhood hope, don't buy the Hallmark version of it -- get down and dirty with the biological version of it THROUGH YOUR BODY. You can dance with your hope - or your hopelessness - by following your heart in movement. See what it evokes.

Heart energy is very much about giving and receiving, and your connection to other humans. Your arms and hands have a natural connection to the heart, and it can be a beautiful thing to imagine this energy extending through your upper limbs as you dance. Remember to connect that with the idea of your lower limbs as roots connecting from the ground up into your heart, grounding and strengthening you, and BAM you'll be unstoppable!

Keep in mind that an overemphasis on dancing from your heart and giving outwards can actually drain your energy if you forget to also get your lower chakras involved. Another client of mine, let's call her Mary, was taking part in my Immersion Workshop and expressed that she was feeling stuck. While trying to come up with creative ideas for turning her recent heartbreak into a solo dance piece, she was coming up against a block. Nothing seemed to flow. It wasn't until I introduced the group to the concept of second chakra hip movement as the house of our creative energy that she realized something.

"I had been trying so hard to dance 'from my heart,' and now I can see that the idea was keeping me stuck because I was ignoring my lower body. I was so focused on giving my energy out and sharing something with other people that I forgot about getting connecting to my own roots first and discovering how it feels in my own body."

Wow. Isn't that cool?

How often do you focus on what something will do for other people, before you truly process it within yourself? (For me? Way too often. It's something I'm getting better at doing, and writing this chapter reinforces it!)

Since more often than not I hear from my clients/students/friends about getting stuck in the patterns of over-giving, I'll encourage you, my dear reader, to take note of your own energy, and much like Mary discovered, check the balance. You may even find it helps you to "follow your heart" more in life. The dance break at the end of this chapter is designed to help you in that process. So ya know what? Enough reading and more moving. Enjoy the dance break and I'll see you in the next chapter.

→ **DANCE BREAK!**

Here's your prompt for this chapter: **Heart Reception**

Start standing in silence with your hands over your heart so that you can potentially hear and feel your own heart beating. Once you get the rhythm, start to tap your hand to match the beat (and if you can't hear it, just create a beat with your hands). Imagine energy circulating from your heart down through your torso, into your legs and feet, and into the ground beneath you. Allow yourself to feel rooted. Then imagine more of that heart energy extending through your arms and hands. As you start to activate your hands, slowly bring them away from your body and open them, palms facing upwards. Hold your arms out in this U shape for a minute as you feel yourself becoming receptive, being able to receive energy and creative inspiration. When you

---

feel complete, return your hands to your heart to bring it to a close. Feel free to take it into more movement if you'd like, playing with the heart energy as it travels through your limbs.

chapter 6: boredom is brilliance.

I t was a Friday night, and I was home alone. My inner dialogue went like this:

Why don't I have a group of friends like the characters on Friends? I should have a Phoebe. Why am I lonely and sad on a Friday night in a city where so much is happening? This is lame. I feel lame. Should I text Allison? Crap, she's not around. Ok, I guess I'll stay here and....

Make a dance video?

That final switch in my thought process changed everything. It was 2012, and Gangnam Style had just gone viral. Inspiration emerged. What if I tried to reshoot the entire music video, scene for scene, with just me and my teddy bear?

And so I did.

And I had so. much. friggin. fun.

(You can still find that video on YouTube as "Jess does Gangnam Style.")

What was responsible for this outpouring of creativity and fun?

Boredom. I owe it all to boredom.

Now, I could have totally gone in another direction with the boredom. I could have numbed myself out with sugar or booze or TV show marathons. And don't get me wrong, sometimes when we're tired or premenstrual, we need to watch the entire second season of *New Girl* all over again because of the "Menzies" episode. But this wasn't the case that Friday night. I wanted to *do* something.

I've since learned that "boredom" is actually just another name for "the fertile void." It's that empty space--the womb, the open container--that's waiting to be filled. The space from which creative babies are born.

It's easy to fall into the trap of thinking that real artists must be creating constantly. Because we live in a produc-tivity-based culture, we believe that we should all be do-ing things constantly. And so we fill our calendars with lots of things to stay "busy," making us feel validated and avoiding all the feelings.

What we forget is that creativity is a cycle, just like every-thing else in life. It needs moments of pause and empty space and not-doing. When you take the time to just be here, that's when the most authentic ideas pop up, seem-ingly out of nowhere. This is why meditation works for so many people - it's a space for the fertile void.

You might be thinking, "Sure, Jess, if I actually had time I'd meditate or be in this void thing you're talking about, but when you work 10 hours a day and have 2 kids and 3 puppies who are all named Poppy who poop a lot, you really don't have time."

Is boredom a luxury?

It might seem like it at first.

I had a pang of guilt pop in even writing this chapter because I'm thinking about all the people in the world - and versions of myself - who "don't have the luxury to be bored" and would kill for a Friday night off to dance around their apartment.

So let me clarify - I'm not saying you need to go on an all-inclusive luxury cruise where the only thing you have to do is be bored and make dance videos. Not at all. I'm saying that even just a little bit of empty time and space - as little as 5 conscious minutes - can open up a new world.

Our society in general has an addiction to being busy, and so many of us fall into that trap. To this day, my mom and Grandma will ask me on the phone, "How are things? *Busy?*" And as soon as the "Yea..." rolls off my tongue the "Well that's goooooood!" response comes shouting through the phone in its Jersey accent. And while busy can be good sometimes, it isn't always -- especially in excess.

What I learned for myself is that being busy is a great excuse for me to not do and be and feel all I'm meant to do and be and feel. "Busy" is an excuse to not write this book, to not step into my true calling, to stay stuck in a cycle of just-getting-by and rushing through life, all so I could avoid my real creative power.

I realized I had been running around, seeking all these outside things to fill the void, rather than simply being with and in the void. These things involved swiping on Bumble (more addictively than intentionally), taking on too much work (that I thought I needed for the money but didn't really want to do), and saying yes to way too many social obligations. (Notice how I just called it a "social obligation." If something feels like an "obligation," it's probably not something you really need to do.)

It took me hauling my ass upstate (to that workshop I mentioned in the introduction) and being out of my normal routine to see all this...to notice where and how I was giving my power and energy away through the very real illusion of busy-ness, and to tap into what was really in my body and soul.

Once I owned that this avoidance was in play and it was keeping me stuck, I started leaning into the void by saying "no" more, by letting go of jobs that weren't truly aligned, and everything shifted a bit. If you're wondering about how I survived or made any money while letting go of jobs, I wondered that too, at first! As it turns out, the creative energy within me is much more money-making than any of the random jobs I was trying to squeeze myself into, and I began making money in ways that felt way more aligned.

I don't mean to position this as one of those stories with a Before and After photo. You know, the ones that make you feel like shit because you're still closer to the Before photo than the After photo. Not at all. I'm still the Before AND the After. Why? Because there actually is no Before and After. There's only the Now. In every moment I have to make the decision to be present with myself and to make choices that are truly aligned with my spirit or to fall back into my old patterns of numbing and avoiding what's true for me. This never ends. Patterns often repeat. Sometimes I go back to saying yes to too many things. Sometimes I question everything. Sometimes I take on a side job because I really do need the extra income. But when I remember to check in with myself, to come back to my body, and to find those small moments of connection through dance, the whole process becomes easier and even fun

To sum it all up, being truly present and allowing some space for the void/boredom/emptiness centers you and gives you your power back. It really only takes one moment - right now - to make that choice.

Before you move on to the next chapter, consider putting the book down and being bored for a few minutes.

→ **DANCE BREAK!**

Here's your prompt for this chapter: **Nothing.**

Set a timer for 15 minutes. Do nothing. Like really, nothing. No phone, no Netflix, no music, no to-do lists. Breathe into whatever uncomfortable feelings might come up as you stare into space and sit with yourself. Pay attention to your body - not just your mind.

---

chapter 7: free yourself.

I had just moved back to Brooklyn after moving to California and back again 6 months later throughout the crumbling of my romantic relationship at the time. I didn't have an apartment and my life was mostly contained in the 1997 Buick Century hand-me-down that was once my Grandpa's. Thanks to the generosity of friends, I had places to stay as I started to rebuild my life.

It was a spring day and I was finally feeling ok. I had signed a lease on a month-long sublet. It felt like a good move to have a space to ground in and figure out my next steps. I was getting all of my stuff out of the car to bring up to this lily pad of a place on Eastern Parkway and slammed the trunk closed only to realize the keys to the car - and the apartment - were inside of the trunk.

[boom crash why am I an idiot f*#@k what did I just do]

The cascade of calling myself an idiot set in and I texted 3 different friends to tell them what an idiot I was. The response that shifted it:

"Why don't you make a dance video until a locksmith gets there?"

Duh, Jess.

With that reframe in mind, I called a locksmith who said he would be there in an hour. I placed my phone camera strategically on a park bench and started dancing out some of the frustration in front of the car. It wasn't long before a crew of construction workers walked by and joined me, and we made an epic dance video and that was that.

My mood went from self-flagellating doom and despair to pure joy and.... freedom.

I had literally locked the keys to my newfound freedom in the trunk of a Buick, and almost believed that was true, until I realized that my creativity was actually where my freedom exists.

It was in me all along.

Note to self:

If you feel trapped, the key to freedom is actually in your body, not the Buick.

Freedom might even be found in the form of a dance video. But this probably won't be obvious at first. The "I'm-an-idiot" voice in your head is likely to speak much louder. It's likely to convince you that you really are an idiot and that this situation is hopeless and that life is so difficult and unfair. You'll say all this to your best friend over the phone while you spoon mint chocolate chip ice cream into your mouth between tears.

We've all been there.

Sometimes all it takes is that friend reminding you that you can choose to do something different. If they have not reminded you, allow me to do the honors.

You have a choice to do something different.

You have a well of creativity inside of you, which, if given a bit of space and attention, can open you up to opportunities and possibilities you might never had known existed.

The best way to give this part of you some space and attention?

Dance.

Dance into your answers, baby.

In creating a visceral experience of freedom, you surrender to something greater. You let go of the tight reigns your brain is holding, as it normally tries to control things or expects a certain kind of outcome. You embrace your body and the emotional/physical/spiritual wisdom that can speak through it when given the chance.

Now, it's important to acknowledge that while we might feel lonely, we are not operating in bubbles separate from the rest of the world. Freeing yourself through dance might not directly free you from the systemic oppression you will encounter. Unfortunately, we live in a world where people are still treated unfairly because of their gender, race, sexual orientation, level of ability, etc. Claiming that dancing alone in your room will free everyone of that crap is a bit idealistic.

BUT. And this is a big but. If you start by freeing yourself through dance, i.e. if you move anxiety and fear through you and out of you, if you start feeling less depressed because you're awakening your body, if you get movement going inside of you, it will be easier to take it outside of yourself. You will be much more likely to have the clarity of mind, energy in your physical body, and confidence in your voice to speak up and create change in the world. It's another version of the "putting on your own oxygen mask first" concept. Take care of you, fill your well of inspiration, release the junk that's holding you back, and you'll be equipped to handle the world and people around you in a much healthier way. On the other hand, if you let yourself get overwhelmed by the plethora of issues in our world and in the news headlines every day, chances are you'll be so frazzled and low that you won't actually do anything. Or you'll try to do EVERYTHING and save EVERYONE and you'll forget about yourself and burn out too quick.

When you start with one step, from a more fulfilled place, you can make progress.

If you don't know where to start, start with a dance. See what freeing yourself with movement does for your state of mind. Then use your mind for the good stuff - the communication that heals, the speaking up for things you believe in, the movements you want to create - rather than the crappy stuff - the worry, the blame, the anxious chatter that will keep you stuck.

One step is all it takes to start.

→ DANCE BREAK!

Here's your prompt for this chapter: **Outside In, Inside Out**

Bring to mind a bigger issue you're grappling with: something in the news headlines, a personal decision, a relationship, etc. As you think about it, notice where in your body feels activated. (Does it bring butterflies to your stomach or lava to your throat?) Allow your body to bring movement to this feeling, and continue to dance it through your system. After your dance, reflect on how it got expressed and what wisdom that movement pattern could bring to your life or to the situation at hand. Then, go take action based on this new learning.

chapter 8: dance alone, together.

"**W**hy does it seem like everyone else is totally into this but all I can think about is my grocery list?"

No, this is not a quote from my latest orgy. (Bummer, right?) It's what was going through my head during a dance class I took. For whatever reason, I couldn't get into the music. I was not finding my flow. And it was a free flowing class, so if I wasn't getting it, why was I there?

After the class, I ended up doing some of my own dancing at home alone, choosing my own music and moving around in my own space which felt like just what I needed. Finding my flow on that particular day had to come from being in my own zone, apparently.

To clarify, it's not that I *only* like to dance alone, or that I'm only recommending you dance alone. There have been plenty of times where I've been really into dancing out in public with others, and sometimes that is exactly the dance medicine I need. If it's the right atmosphere, the collective energy of the group can be inspiring and motivating.

But here's the thing that's worth mentioning -

Whether or not you choose to dance with other people, your solo practice is a keeper. Dancing alone in your room can give you the confidence to dance more in public or to invite friends to join you, if you want. And it can also get you in touch with yourself to know what makes you feel like dancing and what doesn't.

In other words, don't forget about the power of solo dance breaks once you start making more dance friends.

Here's why -

Dancing alone keeps us honest. It gives us space to explore movements we might feel weird about in public. It gives us space to feel like a total rockstar regardless of what others may see. It gives us space to take a trip with ourselves and dance OUR dance for ourselves. Without any outside gaze messin' with us.

After all, you have a unique movement language that wants to be expressed through you, and if you don't give yourself space to explore it, you'll never know what it is. If you don't believe me, maybe you'll believe Martha Graham:

> "There is a vitality, a life force, an energy, a quickening that is translated through you into action, and because there is only one of you in all time, this expression is unique. And if

you block it, it will never exist through any other medium and will be lost.

[*So please listen to Jess.*]'

Italicized portion added by Jess

During a dance break, it's just you...and the music. Or you and the silence, if that's what's feeling powerful for you. This intimacy, this "alone" time, means that you can trust yourself to really let go. To be goofy or sentimental or angry or whatever you want to be while you dance. Whatever you need to be to truly be you.

Solo dance breaks are the space where you can experiment freely without ever worrying if someone is watching you. You can see what it's like to move as YOU, exploring and discovering what that is, without having to measure up to anyone else's movement or expectations.

All that being said, go ahead and try a dance class or go to a crazy dance party. Challenging yourself to dance in other contexts can be great on so many levels. Once you establish a connection with yourself, your ability to connect with others will deepen and your confidence to dance in public will grow -- without needing alcohol to fuel it!

If you're super intimidated but feel kinda ready to get out of your shell, find a dance buddy, i.e. someone to go with you. There's safety in numbers, especially when you're entering a new wild dance jungle full of creatures and movements that you might not be familiar with! Get recommendations from people who've been there first. Drag along your neighbor from down the hall or your friend who always complains about not meeting the right people. Even if the dancing ends up being weird, you'll have stories to tell and you'll move your body a bit. It's a win win.

And remember, if you don't like the context, you can leave. You always have the ability to respectfully excuse yourself from a group dance setting and go do what feels good to YOU (just like I did at that free flowing class I wasn't feeling.) You also have the ability to speak up and help yourself feel more comfortable. Take a moment to chat with the teacher or facilitator beforehand if you can, and let them know you're feeling shy/intimidated/weird/scared and that there's a chance you might want to bow out early. Sometimes simply acknowledging your fear is enough to let it pass and free up your mind so that your body can just dance.

The cool thing is, the more you follow your own rhythm, the more open you'll be to finding a community who has similar taste and values, who you love to dance with, and who loves dancing with YOU. (Because you're pretty cool.)

Depending on where you live, this kind of a dance community could be more or less easy to discover. You'd think that bigger cities would have more options, and they often do, but not always. Even in places like New York City where I live, places where there are TONS of dance classes and events happening each week, I still often hear from people that it's hard to find something that really fits what they're looking for.

If you can relate, follow my recommendations above in finding a dance buddy, and remember that you can also *create* your own dance community. It doesn't have to look like the typical routine of taking a class every week. It could be a communal dance-in-the-park gathering that you facilitate or encouraging your local coffee shop to host a morning dance event once a week. Your solo dance practice can be the foundation that helps you attract others who are drawn to similar dance expressions. Perhaps you start sharing some dance videos (which we'll talk about in the next chapter) and other people see what you're up to and want to join you. (That's what I did years ago, and it's what started the You Can Dance Again movement I cultivated in NYC.) Perhaps you write a message to a bunch of people in your circle and see who might be interested in exploring a dance group together. It could be as simple as inviting a few friends over to your living room, pushing the furniture aside, and having a mini dance party together once a week. It could also look like you hosting an actual dance class or event in your local community.

This process of creating a dance movement that stems from your authentic movement is something I guide people through step by step in my Dance Rebel Leadership Training, by the way. What I've learned from doing this work is that people in cities all over the world have dreams of connecting with people through dance, but it's often our own insecurities and self-doubt that stops us from putting it out there. People *with* dance training often don't feel like they have the right kind of qualifications to teach, or they don't want to repeat the rigid, competitive, structured environment they came from. People *without* dance training often don't feel qualified enough to lead any sort of dance for other people.

What both parties don't realize, in my humble opinion, is that your desire to lead a dance experience in your own authentic way will attract the right people to you, who want exactly what you have to offer. Again, knowing yourself and your solo dance practice is the foundation because it will help you see where you struggle, what you're overcoming through dance, what you are drawn to explore, and that is exactly why others will be drawn to work with you.

I would love to see a world where more dance movements are popping up in this way, where it's not only about learning a particular style of dance, perfecting technique, or getting a workout, but rather freedom of expression, healing, and connectivity through movement.

No matter where your dance path takes you, remember to come home to yourself often. After all, we are always dancing alone, even when we're together. It's in the reflection of each other that we realize dancing alone doesn't have to feel lonely.

→ **DANCE BREAK!**

Here's your prompt for this chapter: Dance Buddy Mirroring.

This one can be done with a fellow dancer, or with a mirror or video. If you have a fellow dancer to try it with, you'll face each other and take turns leading the way with improv. The person not initiating the dance will try to mirror/copy what the other person is doing. After a minute or so, switch roles. See what it's like to try on movement that comes from someone else, and see how it feels to generate your own movement and have it be reflected by someone else. If you don't have a dance buddy available, you can dance in front of a mirror to really see yourself and anchor in your solo dancing. You can also check out the video prompt in my Dance Alone, Together video series, which guides you through doing this exercise along with me in a video!
dancewiththisbook.com

---

chapter 9: the world can watch...or not.

If you've ever bumped into me online, you'll know that I'm a huge fan of making dance videos. For me, there's something about being seen in this way and sharing some of my dancing with others that feels like part of a creative cycle that really wants to move through me.

This might be the same for you, but it doesn't have to be.

Recording yourself while dancing is a choice and it could have different purposes:

- To see how it feels to be witnessed
- To be able to look back and watch what you improvised, gathering ideas for choreography
- To eventually post it somewhere online
- To make a personal keepsake of a particular moment in your life that wants to be remembered in a special way
- To pretend you're starring in a music video

If you just started dancing (again) or if you've never posted a video, it can be a delicate, vulnerable thing to do. Hell, it's a delicate and vulnerable thing even if you've been doing it for years! So be gentle and compassionate with your process and be very picky about who gets to see the videos - at first.

One of the reasons I've been drawn to making dance videos is because of the shared expression inherent in it. When I first started getting back to my dance practice after years away from it, I needed time to just dance on my own and know that no one was watching. Then I noticed a desire emerge to take the movement I was experiencing, create something with it, and share it. Much in the same way a dance performance is giving something to the audience who sees it, making a dance video is giving something to the people who view it. It's a release of creative expression which will be received by someone else, who will then take it in as inspiration and hopefully express it out again at some point, in some other form, to pass it on. Your dance video might make someone feel an emotion they've long held buried inside, whether it's a chuckle or tears or even anger and jealousy because it makes them realize that they also miss dancing and regret not doing more of it. You don't have control over other people's reactions, you only have the responsibility to move the creative energy through your body and out into the world.

The act of recording a dance can bring up a lot for you, too. It's an aspect of being witnessed, and allowing yourself to be seen by others which can be challenging. All sorts of hangups made themselves present when I started posting my dance videos: Does this seem egotistical? (i.e. who am I to be posting my dance videos?) What will people think? Am I allowed to present myself as "a dancer" even though it's been so many years since I've done it and I have a "real job?" Will people judge me for being "out of shape?" Will no one even acknowledge it and I'll feel like a loser for trying to share it in the first place?

Somehow I made the choice to hit publish despite these concerns, and I'm happy I did because the level of connection it brought to my life outweighed all of the negative aspects.

From an artistic standpoint, making a dance video is an act of preserving an art form that is normally so transient. There's nothing like seeing live dance, of course, but with video we get to capture a bit of its essence. I used to be jealous of other artists like painters and poets who got to create such tangible pieces that would live on after them. Dance videos have since become my version of that. Short movement poems that can be witnessed again, even if it's just for yourself, to remember aspects of who you are and to continue sharing moments with others.

Whether or not you choose to share your dance videos with the world at large, they could be poignant keepsakes for your own process, like a video dance journal that reminds you of where you're coming from and how you're evolving.

And remember, this whole video thing is totally totally optional!

If you do have an impulse to share, know WHY you are sharing it.

Is it coming from a place of hoping to get approval or a lot of likes on Instagram?

Is it coming from a place of fun, humor, sadness, or joy?

Is it coming from your heart and soul or your head?

Check in with yourself.

It's ok to want to people to like it - there's nothing wrong with you if you do. In fact, it's a pretty common desire. We all want to be loved. But if you're posting a video ONLY because you want it to be liked, or if you feel yourself getting crushed and down on yourself when it doesn't get liked as much as you'd hoped for, then it might be time to take a step back and pause the posting for a bit until you can remember the whole reason you're doing this anyway is because YOU find joy in it. You love yourself enough to make time and space for what brings you joy. That's got to be at the center of all this, or it will just feel heavy and off.

I say this from experience. Recently during my annual Dance-a-Day in the Month of May challenge, I found myself getting burnt out and not excited about the idea of making a dance video each day. That year I had challenged myself to not just dance daily but to dance *with other people* every single day. I thought I was challenging myself to step out of my comfort zone with this idea, and I did because it got me talking to new people and making some cool stuff. But then it started to feel heavy. I thought that if I broke my commitment and just danced alone that people would think I'm a flake and I'd be letting them down.

When I gave myself permission to say "F that" and I danced alone in a hallway on Day 27, I suddenly felt free again. I realized that my intention to dance with people and make bigger, more exciting dance videos was coming from a place of me not feeling enough. I thought it wasn't enough for me to record myself dancing alone (which is ironic, because the whole way I started dancing again after so much time away from it was by dancing alone in my room). This realization not only freed my dancing, but it spurred a new program idea, and later, this whole book. I'm not joking. Letting go of trying to win everyone's approval and getting back to the origin of making dance videos alone in my room literally created the current version of this book. Hence, the whole focus on returning to that sacred act of dancing alone in your room.

We'll cover more on approval-seeking in the next chapter, and until then, I invite you to get your video camera on and give the video shoot a shot!

→ **DANCE BREAK!**

Here's your prompt for this chapter: Make a Dance Video.

Just for kicks, try recording yourself dancing. Give yourself permission to mess up, as usual, as well as permission to delete the video if you want afterwards. Notice what having a camera on you does to your dance. If you do decide to post it, please tag me - @jessgrippo and #dancewiththisbook - so that I can see it and cheer you on!

INVITATION:

Want a deeper dive into dance-video-making? I created an online training course just for that purpose. The video making itself can be a fantastic creative outlet as you learn to play with edits and lighting and music. It can also be a great visibility tool to share your art or your work with others, if that's something you desire. In this video course you'll learn the technical basics of shooting and editing your own videos - no experience necessary! -and reach more people authentically. If you'd like to check it out, there's a special insider rate for book readers which you can access over at the digital companion: dancewiththisbook.com

chapter 10: my mother thinks you're great.

A few years ago, my dance partner Ben was posting a bunch of dance videos, as he does, and we had a running joke to see if anyone would outdo my mother in being the first one to like it or comment. Most of the time, Sue Grippo won. (That's my Moms.) I can list a bunch of friends who can attest to Mama Grippo's supportive, enthusiastic Facebook-liking habits, often accompanied by a comment that ends in an exclamation point! ("Just fabulous!")

In other words, if you ever feel down on yourself or not good enough, friend my mother on Facebook. Her name is Susan Grippo. I got her permission. This woman is everyone's biggest fan.

I say that jokingly, but also for real.

When you hold yourself back from doing something creative or dancing, think about my mom scrolling through Facebook and waiting to see something inspiring. Think about my mom saying "woo!" loudly and clapping right before she hits the "like" button. Think of my mom who has been a caretaker for my father for the last 7+ years after a debilitating stroke, who went through treatment for and survived stage 3 breast cancer and stage 4 melanoma at the same time, who is one of the strongest women I know - to a fault, at times.

She wants to, needs to see your creative energy coming through the screen so that she can be reminded of her own. And she doesn't just like your posts because she feels obligated to, she likes them because she sees what you're doing as a true miracle.

That's how I want you to see yourself.

(And of course, Mom, that's how I want YOU to see yourself.)

Now, here's the trap. I'm not saying you should ONLY see yourself as a miracle IF my mother likes your post. You are a miracle no matter what she or anyone else says or does. Approval seeking can become a drug. If you find yourself double-checking (or quintuple-checking) social media posts to see the status of likes received, chances are, you are an approval seeker. (Haiiiiiii. Welcome to the club.)

Chances are your mother or father didn't give you enough approval, or gave you conditional approval - as in, you only felt loved when you performed well in school or won a soccer game. I'm not a therapist, but I am a coach and I thought this was worth mentioning. If you get really emotional reading this OR if you feel totally numb, it might be worth talking to your therapist or coach about it. (And if you don't have one, reach out.)

Here's something that might help in the meantime.

Instead of looking to my mother or your mother for approval, let's turn our attention to the Great Mother. The maker of rain and sun and also rainbows. The Mother who is with us always, even when we choose to ignore her and drink Starbucks and feel guilty after throwing out the disposable cup, imagining how many thousands of those get thrown out every day and litter the planet.

I'm talking about Mama Earth, the Great Goddess we live on. If that's too hippie-dippy for you, I'm talking about Mother Nature. If *that's* too hippie-dippy for you, I'm not sure why you're reading this book because I am quite a bit hippie-dippy once you get to know me. Maybe this chapter will make you feel more comfortable with what all that crap is about anyway.

So why am I talking about earthly goddess stuff in a book about dance? Well, dance involves our BODIES and our bodies are connected to the earth. And the moon. If you're someone who menstruates, your cycle is influenced by the tides of the moon each month. If you're not, your body is 80% water and still influenced. The seasons around us are cyclical, too, and all of that affects how we feel, think, and act - whether we know it or not.

I also bring this up here because if you can tap into this ever-present energy around us in nature, you might find relief from approval-seeking. You might just remember that you are one with nature. She is supporting you. She is literally holding you here on your feet or butt by the forces of gravity. She's not letting go. You are ok. You are more than ok - here's that reminder again -

You are a miracle.

No matter what your mama or someone else's mama has said or done, Mama Earth is ever loving and will help restore you. If you've ever found solace in being by the ocean, you'll know what I mean.

Tapping into more of this energy - maybe through actually going to the ocean more, or going to the park, or spending time with puppies or trees - will without a doubt help you feel more grounded. From that place, you can mother yourself the way you've always wished you were mothered. You can approve of yourself. You can like your own Facebook posts if you want! Do what it takes to love and approve of yourself and watch your world transform.

The miracle is in you. Mama said so.

→ DANCE BREAK!

Here's your prompt for this chapter: **Self-Approval Applause**

This one's all about approving of yourself. Create an imaginary audience to start. You can draw some stick figures on post-it notes and stick it to your wall, or line up your kid's stuffed animals, or just create them with your imagination. Look into their eyes and see a loving, approving gaze. Set the intention that this audience is there to cheer you on and be wowed by whatever you choose to do. Then put on a song that makes you feel amazing. (My personal choices here, in honor of our theme, would be Lady Gaga's "Applause" or Hot Chocolate's "You Sexy Thing".) Dance it out. Be witnessed by this loving, approving audience. Listen to the (imaginary) applause after. Then applaud yourself - literally. Clap your hands together and then clap your hands all over your body as you tap yourself full of approval. Once you're complete, stand in silence and take in the energy. Feel your body becoming receptive to love and approval and notice how it makes you feel.

chapter 11: self-expression is not selfish.

G uess what?
It's not about you.

That might sound strange, because you probably found this book in the self-help section.

But hey, isn't it a relief to take some pressure off?

Lemme guess -

You've probably felt guilty for taking time for yourself to dance because it felt too "selfish."

You've probably stopped yourself from posting a dance video or sharing your art because you thought no one would care about something that YOU did when so much else is happening in the world.

Or maybe you've worried about what Marge from the office would think of you if you posted that thing on Instagram. (Scandalous! Marge, check out the nerve in that one!)

In all these cases, you're essentially making everything about You, under the guise of being worried about what Everyone Else thinks. I know this because I'm really good at doing this, too. In fact, I probably wrote this chapter for myself because I still get caught in these patterns.

One of the main reasons I decided to quit dance at 19-years-old was I felt a desire to help people, and at the time, dancing ballet felt too "selfish" to me. I couldn't see how I'd be making any impact on the world by pursuing something I was passionate about that would keep me locked in a dance studio all day long. So I did what many young people do when they have a desire to help people but don't know how - I studied psychology. That path eventually led me to holistic health, which eventually led me back to dance, which came full circle when I realized part of my calling was to help people *through dance*, which had to happen by first reconnecting to dance myself.

Here's what I want to remind us both -

When you stop yourself from the natural impulse of self-expression, you're most likely putting yourself in the brains of Everyone Else and imagining what they will think and say about You, so you're wasting a lot of energy imagining other people care enough about what the hell you're doing. We don't got time for that. The world don't got time for that.

Taking moments for "selfish" acts like dancing alone in your room is, in fact, a really responsible, healthy form of self-care. It goes back to what we talked about in the Free

Yourself chapter: putting on the metaphorical oxygen mask before you help others with theirs.

Expressing yourself and refueling your creative tank is going to allow you to give more, do more, and be more of The Real You in all areas of your life. It's just a fact. It doesn't mean that making time to dance again will end up making dance a huge part of your career - but it could if you want to. The point is to nurture your creative self and let it show you the way.

Instead of being worried about Everyone Else's thoughts about you, how about shifting your concern to the greater health of humanity? How about you remember that creative expression heals us, that dancing is medicine, that the world is starving for more of this kind of medicine? How about you remember your body is a vessel that is wired to express itself, and every time you block it, you're blocking the flow of nature itself? (Nature has enough blockages due to our modern lifestyle, so let's not add to that mess, ok?)

In letting yourself dance and express yourself, you are letting something else speak through you. You are simply the channel through which the creative muses speak. And you're delivering an important message. You're putting inspiration back into the cyclical creative well so someone else can pick it up and feed off your expression. Dancing is both medicinal and contagious - go figure!

So while it's not about you, it is up to you to keep your dance alive and to keep your creative channel open because it truly will make a difference in how you show up in the world. In my opinion, it should be a civil duty, a workplace requirement, that everyone must dance daily. Imagine that?

As Gandhi said, "Let's be the change we wish to see in the world." Be dance.

→ **DANCE BREAK!**

Here's your prompt for this chapter: **Dedicated Dance.**

Let today's dance embody the contagious chain of inspiration. Start by thinking about a musical artist whose self-expression inspires you, uplifts you, helps you to feel less alone, etc. Play one of their songs and feel gratitude for this act of self-expression that one human created at one point, which can feel healing and nourishing to you, another human, in this separate moment right now. Soak this in. Then, think of someone in your life who you love and who could use a boost of inspiration. Dance to this same song while dedicating it to that person, and pass on the healing chain of self-expression.

---

chapter 12: dance away with your true self.

As we bring this baby to a close, I feel a mix of excitement with a tinge of sadness. I've always enjoyed beginnings much more than endings. But alas, every ending IS a new beginning.

This is YOUR new beginning.

Perhaps you're feeling a mix of things, too. Because now, it's time to stop reading and to start dancing, if you haven't yet.

I hope the elements of this book have done a great job of re-inspiring you to dance again and have given you the practical tools necessary to bust through anything that's stopping you from making it happen.

Now it's up to you to dance YOUR dance.

It's up to you to dance for no other reason than because you want to and your soul is calling you to do it.

Not because anyone else is telling you to. Not "someday" when you get into that company, or when a class opens up near your house, or when you lose ten pounds...

You can dance NOW. In the beautiful body you live in, wherever you live, and in whatever phase of life you find yourself.

Remember this -

Your body is meant to move and speak and dance through life.

When those random impulses to dance strike, follow them!

Dance is way more than being able to kick your leg up high or do those fancy flip moves you see people doing on *So You Think You Can Dance*.

Dance is more about what's inside of you than what your outside form does.

Dance will not only free you in the moment you're dancing, but it will free you in your life as it lifts and shifts your mood and helps you feel more connected to yourself and to others.

So don't wait for someone to give you permission. If you feel the need for some kind of validation, take this book as the sign you've been searching for.

Here's to dancing into our answers in unexpected places and transforming ourselves and our world through the very thing that makes us human: our ability to create, express, and dance.

'Nuff said. Get to it.

→ **DANCE BREAK!**

Here's your prompt for this chapter: **Own it.**

Say this out loud: "I'm a dancer. I'm a dance rebel!"
Say it again. And one more time. Then put on some
music and do a celebration dance for yourself and
the reclaiming of this powerful part of you.

HERE'S YOUR PERMISSION SLIP

(feel free to rip this page out and hang it up on your wall)

I, _____, can dance again.

(in my own way, in the body I have right now, even if I'm very busy.)

I now have permission. not that I needed it, but hey, a little encouragement can be a catalyst.

Signed: _____

chapter 13: keep it movin'.

I'm going to guess that there are so many possibilities for your creative life – beyond what you or I could think up in this moment – that will emerge naturally as you begin to dance more on your own.

What I want to leave you with is the idea that YOU get to make the rules in your dance world. It's up to you to decide which elements of dance you choose to include in your life and how they all cook together.

To help you in that process, I'm including some of my own offerings and resources that could support you (including both online and in person options, listed at the end of the chapter!), plus a whole series of bonus dance prompts that can assist your personal dance practice.

Let's start by getting clear on which elements of dance you'd like to keep or add to your life. Turn the page for a fill-in-the-blanks Dance Recipe...

_____'S DANCE RECIPE

INGREDIENTS *(check all that apply)*

- ☑ daily dance breaks
- ☑ taking dance classes: _____
- ☑ personal studio space rental*(___ days per month)*
- ☑ dance video making
- ☑ teaching dance
- ☑ choreographing dances
- ☑ performing my own work
- ☑ performing other people's choreography
- ☑ auditioning for a show or company
- ☑ dancing socially
- ☑ other: _____

QUESTIONS TO CONSIDER:

How often will each ingredient show up? (add them to your calendar if you can!)

Do I want collaborators or community? Who?

What am I uncertain or unclear about? What am I curious to discover?

Would I like to stay connected to Jess and the Dance Rebel community?

BONUS DANCE PROMPTS

In addition to the prompts listed at the end of each chapter in this book, I wanted to provide you with a few extras and point you in the direction of some resources that could support your dance practice.

I know sometimes it can be hard to dance randomly without any guidance at all, whether you're brand new to dance breaks or if you've been doing them for a while. Sometimes you might feel blank, not knowing exactly what to do or how to move, and other times, you might get bored with the movements you routinely fall into and the music you usually pick. All of this is totally normal, I promise. Even for the seasoned dance-breaker, a way to shake things up is necessary, and that's where these prompts come in!

If you're feeling stuck, bored, blah, whatever, I've been where you are. I've created these guided dance prompts while moving through my own stuff and I've used them successfully, both for myself and with my clients and students. Utilizing prompts is a great way to keep the dancing fresh and inspired. And if you're someone who teaches dance to others, these could be utilized in your classes, too!

(If you do use them in your classes, which I encourage you to do freely, please give credit to this book. :)

PROMPTS MOSTLY FOR THE SAKE OF MOVEMENT:

"Wait for it" – Either with or without music, start by standing in total stillness. Allow yourself to pause and breathe and wait in stillness until something in your body stirs you to move. In other words, don't move because you think you should, but really try to find the movement that's being called from your physical body. You can also set the intention to let the stillness become part of your dance. You can explore what might be moving inside of you when you're not engaging more actively with your body. Give yourself permission to pause at any time, and wait for it. Wait for the stir from within to propel your dance. (As in dance and as in life: even in the moments where life seems to stand still or we feel stuck, there is always so much stirring beneath the surface.)

"Magnet" – Imagine there's a magnet inside of you. Where does it live in your body and how does it make you dance? Do you draw things towards you, or are you magnetized toward the objects around you? Bonus: as you're dancing with your eyes closed, imagine that the magnet is drawing you closer to specific things in life that you're currently desiring.

"Shake Break" – Shake and shimmy every body part, and then spend some time shaking your whole body at once. Imagine letting go of stale of energy or anything and everything you no longer need. Bonus: do this for longer than is "comfortable." Start using discomfort in this contained space to discover your edges. Often there is gold to be found beyond the point that we usually stop ourselves.

PROMPTS TO SPARK YOUR IMAGINATION:

"The Weird Ugly Dance" – Give yourself permission to dance freely, releasing any pressure you feel to make it look beautiful or "good." Make the dance as weird or as ugly as you possibly can. This one is especially powerful for my fellow type-A-ers out there who might be consciously or subconsciously always trying to create "beautiful" movement. Let your monster side out, let your freak flag fly, and let your inner child throw a tantrum party. You might be surprised at what comes out of it!

"The Imaginary Friend" – Imagine a dance partner is standing right next to you. Or grab your nearest Teddy Bear and have them play the part. Put on your favorite love song or heartbreak song and dance with your imaginary partner. How do you wish someone would dance with you? Are there elements of loneliness or longing that are asking to be expressed? How can inspiration from an imaginary object inspire more love for yourself? These are the kind of questions that can be explored within this prompt.

"The Pop Star" – Simply stated, channel your favorite pop star. Sing and dance along to their songs. Dress up and grab a microphone if you'd like. This is perfect for those moments when your confidence feels fizzled and you are craving a boost in your playfulness, sexiness, or overall energy. It's a great reminder to not take things so seriously. By emulating someone you admire, you get to also discover how those qualities they possess actually live and dance in you, too.

PROMPTS THAT PROVIDE INSIGHT INTO LIFE:

"Move Through It" – Start out on one side of the room, and dance a pathway to the other side. Imagine that the place you start is where you are in your life right now and that the place you're headed is a specific goal or feeling you desire to move into. Dance your way through, paying attention to how it feels to get there, what kind of resistance you encounter, and how you feel called to move through it...essentially breaking through any challenges that might cross your path. Afterward, reflect on your experience and write or feel into how it can inform your current life situation.

"The Anger Dance" – Get some music that riles you up. (Think: Rage Against the Machine.) Make sure you're in a place where it's ok to be loud, and if you have downstairs neighbors, let them know they might hear some banging. Then let 'er rip! Turn on your music, as loud as feels good to you (louder than normal!), and stomp, scream, shake, punch pillows...do whatever your body wants to do to release some anger. If you're going through a situation in your life that's bringing up a lot of anger, it's great to precede this dance prompt by writing an angry letter to express what you're feeling. (You won't send this letter to anyone, so feel free to write uncensored. Then, I highly recommend tearing, crumbling, and stomping on the letter as part of the dance. You can also choose to burn it or flush it down the toilet afterwards, in a ritualistic act of fully letting go.) While it might feel uncomfortable and scary to express your anger at first, it's super healthy and freeing to let these emotions be expressed. I adapted this prompt from what I learned back in my days as a health coach with Flo Living, where we would conduct an entire day-long workshop on healthy expressions of anger!

PROMPTS FOR WHEN YOU'RE NOT FEELING SUPER CREATIVE:

"Tell-Me-What-To-Do" – For the days when you don't have the creative drive to freestyle, let someone else tell you what to do. Search for "dance classes" on YouTube and pick one that looks like fun. You could also ask via your social media channels to get suggestions from friends. You can also try mirroring someone else's dance video (i.e. watching someone's choreography or improv and trying to match their movements, doing it along with them). Letting others guide your movement sometimes is a great way to stimulate your creativity and get you moving in ways you might not normally move. During the improv/freestyle segments of my live dance classes, I often invite the dancers to observe one another and borrow movements from each other, trying on what someone else's movement would feel like. It's a great antidote for boredom or getting stuck in the rut of doing the same type of dance over and over again. And, it's cool to see how the same movement can be interpreted differently by different bodies.

NEXT LEVEL PROMPTS THAT ARE HELPFUL WHEN CHOREOGRAPHING OR CREATING:

Start with what you know – If you don't know where to start, start with something you know. Pick a dance move you already do and start doing it on repeat or as the anchor to a series of movements. See where it takes you as you allow the movement to naturally evolve into something else, or keep coming back to this one movement as your anchor. (My personal fave is the opening sequence of "All That Jazz".... Head roll. Paint the town.)

Let the music guide you – Using the same sequence of movements (a short phrase that you already know or one that you create on the spot), try dancing these movements to different song choices. Or go back to the trusty Dance Shuffle method from Chapter 2's dance break! Hit shuffle and let the music move you. Notice how different musical genres, rhythms, or melodies - or even silence - influence how the movements feel and how you are drawn to execute them. Play and see what lights up your process.

Mix up your media – Collect a few objects, excerpts of text or poetry, or images that inspire you, and use them in the dance studio. With physical objects, try holding the object and dancing with it. Then try pretending that you ARE the object and dance as you imagine it would move. For images, visualize the essence of it and dance through it. Read the text out loud as you move, or create a movement phrase influenced by key words in the text.

So there you have it. A few structured ways to play with your movement and get yourself dancing and creating.

I'm a huge fan of dance prompts because we are not meant to create in a bubble. Invitations, structured guidance, and specific parameters to begin with can all open up endless possibilities.

And speaking of not dancing in a bubble, I'd love for you to join me online or in person for the various community dance events and programs I host:

- Revive your personal dance practice and your creative spark through my 1-1 coaching programs and **You Can Dance Again** group program offerings.
- Create a movement with your movement via **The Dance Rebel Leadership Training**, a course I created to help spread more authentic dance movements across the globe by guiding you in creating and launching your own local dance class/event/program.
- Join the Facebook group **"The Dance Rebels' Collective"** to find fellow dance rebels and take part in the live dance challenges I host, including

the much-loved annual Dance a Day in the Month of May.

There are always new things being born, so check out the general website for links to all of the above and more, and follow the journey on Instagram:

<u>jessgrippo.com</u> | <u>@jessgrippo</u>

Dance on, my friend.

You can dance again.

You can dance when you're happy,
You can dance when you're sad.
You can dance when that burger
Was the best you ever had.

You can dance when it's rainy,
You can dance in the sun.
You can dance with a stranger,
And even with a nun.

You can dance in a minute,
You can dance in an hour.
You can dance in your sorrow
Or to find your hidden power.

You can dance to free your body,
You can dance to find an answer.
You dance whether or not
You think you are a dancer.

You can dance to go crazy,
You can dance to get real zen.
And even if you choose to stop,
You can always dance again.

- Jess Grippo

gratitude

I am so deeply thankful to the dance rebels of the past who have paved the way for me and so many others to do our work. Among some of whom have inspired me (and this is not a comprehensive list, for there are too many to name) -- Agnes De Mille, Loie Fuller, Josephine Baker, Isadora Duncan, Pina Bausch, Gwen Verdon. I recognize that dance, like any art form, is a borrowed medium, one that is recycled through generations. It is with a deep, humble bow that I honor my dance ancestors who moved this energy through their bodies, who danced to literally survive, at a time when it might have been dangerous to do so. I honor those who have passed through history unnamed, but no doubt have inspired me and set the foundation for more dance to move through us.

To my personal mentors and kindred spirits - in the dance world and beyond - who have helped guide my path: Vinny Pici, Alisa Vitti, Erin Malley, Mark Seltman, Master Jey Park, Joanna Lindenbaum, Dawn Copeland, Kyle Cease, Dieufel Lamisere, David Horne, Pete SennYuen, Jeffrey at the coffee shop. And to the authors who have inspired my creative path: Julia Cameron, Steven Pressfield, Austin Kleon, Elizabeth Gilbert, Amanda Palmer. Thank you for your work and for inspiring mine.

To my local Brooklyn dance studio owners who have welcomed me into your home and given me a reason to not always dance alone in my room: Renee Manzolillo at Breakin Boundaries, Maya Jocelyn at Studio Maya, and Valerie Wright at Brooklyn Center Stage. Thank you for the studio space and for the encouragement.

To my original You Can Dance Again community who trusted me enough to step into the studio for the first time -- I do not take that for granted. To Cate Prefontaine Hausmann and Michelle Maso who have stuck with it since the beginning and have carried on the torch with your own amazing dance leadership and choreography. To every single person who has opened an email from me, liked a dance video I posted, pre-ordered this book (and waited 3 years! thanks for your patience!) or was inspired to take a personal dance break for yourself, thank you so much for being here. I hope you continue to dance.

To my family of origin and chosen family: the early artistic inspiration of my Great Aunt Marianne who made me realize that my artistic path could be valid, my "All That Jazz" partner for life Allison Joyce who is always willing to throw on a tutu at a moment's notice, my little cousins and adopted nieces/nephews who continue to show me what dance and life is really about, and my mother and father who let me follow my crazy dance path even when they didn't understand it. Thank you forever.

To Sasha Mercedes and Sally Mercedes, who have worked with me in many forms over the last seven years, whose support, guidance, and belief in me and my business this year ultimately created the space to be able to finish this book. Thank you for being there, even when it wasn't easy.

To my book doula and line editor Tyla Fowler who did so much more than make sense of my words. Thank you for helping to midwife this book into existence through the various forms it's taken on. Really couldn't have done it without you. To my copyeditor Niki Carlotti who took care with these words and helped me complete a long overdue process. Thank you for believing in it. And thank you both for reviving YOUR dance along the way.

I am honored and humbled to be able to dance freely in this world and do not take it for granted. While the movement of my work glides on humor and joy at times, it's foundation is deeply rooted in the shared pain of humanity with hopes that we can heal and grow together into a more connected, loving, dance-filled world.

P.S. DID YOU DANCE WITH ME?

If so, please share! Share your videos while dancing with this book on social media with this hashtag so that we can cheer each other on:

#dancewiththisbook

If it *really* moved you, feel free to leave a review on the website where you bought it, or directly to this inbox: jess@jessgrippo.com

Would be thrilled to hear from you!

And remember, I'm here for you anytime you need a dance boost.

Love,

This Book

Made in the USA
San Bernardino, CA
16 December 2019